SAVING WOLVES

Wolves Discovery Library

Lynn M. Stone

The Rourke Book Company, Inc.
Vero Beach, Florida 32964

PHOTO CREDITS
© Lynn M. Stone: cover, title page, p.4, 14–15, 17, 18, 20;
© Thomas Kitchin: p.7;
© David Mech: p.8, 10,11, 13;
© Deborah Sussex/International Wolf Center: p.12;
courtesy National Park Service: p.16

EDITORIAL SERVICES
Penworthy Learning Systems

Library of Congress Cataloging-in-Publication Data

Stone, Lynn M.
Saving wolves / Lynn Stone.
p. cm. — (Wolves discovery library)
Summary: Discusses reasons that wolves were almost hunted out of existence in the United States and efforts to reintroduce these animals to certain areas of the northern United States.
ISBN 1-55916-240-6
1. Wolves—Juvenile literature. 2. Wildlife conservation—Juvenile literature. [1. Wolves. 2. Wildlife conservation.] I. Title.

QL737.C22 S766 2000
599.773—dc21
00-020871

Printed in the USA

CONTENTS

THE BIG, BAD WOLF?

Big and beautiful, wolves are living **symbols** of wild places. In North America, these biggest members of the dog family have become a favorite of wild animal lovers. But wolves haven't always been loved.

Europeans who settled in North America didn't like wolves or any other big **predator**, or hunter. Settlers feared that wolves would harm them and kill their farm animals. They also didn't like sharing their wild game, like deer and elk, with wolves.

American settlers shot, trapped, and poisoned wolves. They also killed off much of the wolves' wild **prey**.

Wolves are a living symbol of the North American wilderness. No one who has heard a wolf's howl forgets it.

SAVING THE WOLF

Wolves vanished wherever towns and farms appeared. By the early 1970s, the only major wolf population south of Canada was in northern Minnesota. But by then, people's feelings toward wolves had begun to change. Most people were smart enough not to see wolves as "good" or "bad." People began to learn more about wolves from scientists. The old tales about big, bad wolves were shown to be foolish.

The U.S. Congress passed the Endangered Species Act in 1973. The Act was a series of laws. They gave protection to plants and animals that were threatened with **extinction**. An animal **species**, or kind, is extinct if all of its members are destroyed.

Wolves were nearly gone from the lower 48 states by 1970. Today they are found in nine states outside Alaska.

Dr. David Mech watches Arctic wolves on Ellesmere Island. The wolf studies led by Dr. Mech in the 1960s and 1970s helped gather public support for wolves.

The wolf wasn't in danger of becoming extinct. It was, however, in danger of being pushed completely out of the lower 48 states. That allowed the U.S. Government to put the wolf under its protection.

WOLF SCIENCE

In the early 1940s, Adolph Murie made a careful and thoughtful study of wolves in Denali National Park, Alaska. His efforts led to further studies by such men as Durward Allen, Rolph Peterson, Lou Carbyn, and David Mech.

In the 1960s, scientists began to capture wolves and fit them with radio collars. Scientists could pick up signals from the radios. The scientists could then follow the wolves by radio contact. Scientists also began to study captive packs of wolves.

Wolf **research**, or study, continues. Research has helped the public to know the real wolf.

This Alaskan wolf has been drugged by a dart. Now the wolf can be fitted for a radio collar.

A signal to this wolf's radio collar released a knock-out drug. Now scientists can measure the wolf, check its health, and release it.

The International Wolf Center in Ely, Minnesota, draws thousands of visitors each year. The Center teaches about wolf behavior and conservation.

Scientists can receive signals from a wolf's radio collar. Scientists can also send signal to the collar.

The wolf the public knows today is not the fearsome one in fairy tales and **myths**.

People now know the wolf as more than just a hunter of big mammals. Thanks to science and photography, people know about the wolf's personality and amazing family structure. Wolves in packs hunt, eat, rest, play, nap, and raise pups together.

Many people once believed that wolves killed far more animals than they could eat. Wolves rarely kill more than they need.

RETURNING WOLVES TO NATURE

With help, the wolf is returning to the northern United States. The U.S. Fish and Wildlife Service calls its program "wolf recovery." The idea is to make sure that wolves are returned to at least some of the wild places where they used to live.

For example, U.S. Government trappers killed off the last wolves in Yellowstone National Park in 1926. In 1995, the government made right that old wrong. It released 31 Canadian wolves in Yellowstone. Many ranchers were not happy. They howled more loudly than the wolves. They feared attacks on their livestock if wolves trotted out of the park.

Onlookers watch as a truck brings wolves into Yellowstone National Park for release.

Another group of wolves was released into a wilderness area in Idaho. Idaho ranchers and state **lawmakers** complained. The Nez Perce tribe, however, wanted the wolf release. It agreed to take over Idaho's wolf recovery program.

The number of wolves in Yellowstone and in Idaho continues to grow. Minnesota's wolf population is around 2,000, up from 600 in the 1950s. Michigan and Wisconsin have a small but growing number of wolves. Wolves from the Canadian Rocky Mountains have spread into Glacier National Park, Montana.

Mexican gray wolves released in New Mexico in the late 1990s have not been welcomed by all of the state's ranchers.

THE WOLF'S FUTURE

Wolves still face angry ranchers and lawmakers who side with them. Some hunters' groups also dislike having wolves compete with them for game animals.

But the wolf's future in the northern United States is bright. Wolves may some day be returned to the Olympic Peninsula in Washington, the Adirondack Mountains of New York, and the north woods of New Hampshire and Maine.

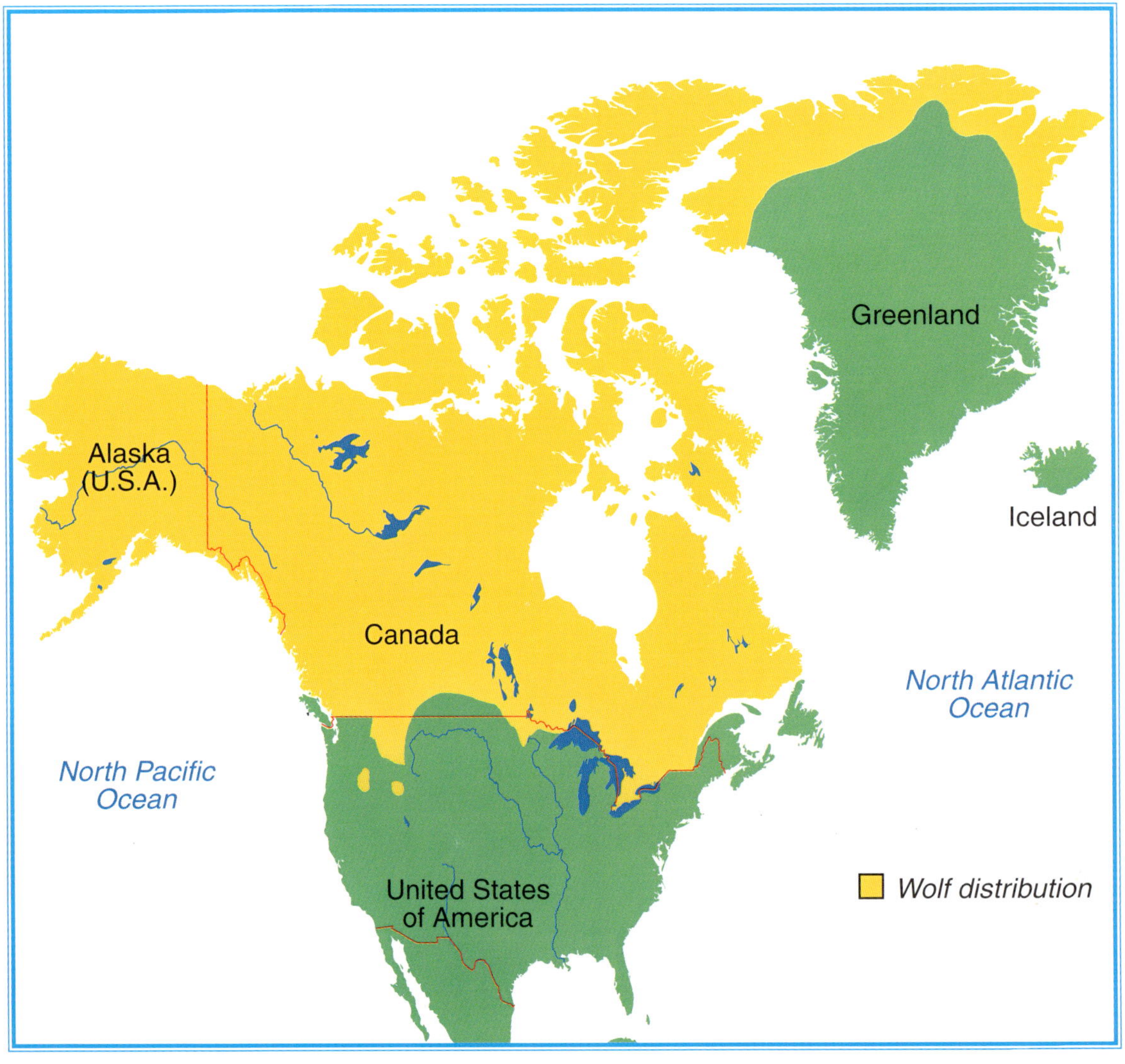
Greenland
Iceland
Alaska
(U.S.A.)
Canada
North Atlantic
Ocean
North Pacific
Ocean
United States
of America
Wolf distribution

GLOSSARY

extinction (ik STINGK shuhn) – the state, or condition, of a kind of animal no longer existing

lawmakers (LAW may ker) – those people (politicians) such as senators and representatives, who are elected to consider and pass laws

myth (MITH) – an often repeated story or tale which is not true, but is often believed

predator (PRED uh ter) – an animal that hunts and kills other animals for food

prey (PRAY) – an animal that is hunted for food by another animal

research (REE serch) – the information (knowledge) that is gathered from careful scientific study; to gather new information in an orderly way

species (SPEE sheez) – within a group of closely related animals, such as deer, one certain type (mule deer)

symbol (SIM buhl) – a sign or representation of something else

FURTHER INFORMATION

Find out more about wolves with these helpful books and websites:

International Wolf Center on line at www.wolf.org

Lawrence, R.D. **Wolves**. Sierra Club, 1990

Patent, Dorothy Hinshaw. **Gray Wolf Red Wolf**. Clarion, 1990

Swinburne, Stephen. **Once a Wolf**. Houghton Mifflin, 1999

INDEX